The Art & Design Series

For beginners, students, and working professionals in both fine and commercial arts, these books offer practical how-to introductions to a variety of ideas in contemporary art and design. Each illustrated volume is written by a working artist, a specialist in his or her field, and each concentrates on an individual area—from advertising layout or printmaking to interior design, printing, and cartooning, among others. Each contains information that artists will find useful in the studio, in the classroom, and in the marketplace. Among the books in the series:

An Introduction to Design:
Basic Ideas and Applications
for Paintings or the Printed Page
Robin Landa

Graphic Design:
A Problem-Solving Approach to Visual Communication
Elizabeth Resnick

Display Design:
An Introduction to Window Display,
Point-of-Purchase, Posters, Signs and Signage,
Sales Environments, and Exhibit Displays
Laszlo Roth

A Concise Guide to Graphic Arts and Printing for Small Businesses and Nonprofit Organizations

IN PRINT

Mindy N. Levine
with Susan Frank

A Spectrum Book
Prentice-Hall, Inc., Englewood Cliffs, N.J. 07632

Library of Congress Cataloging in Publication Data

Levine, Mindy N., 1955—
  In print.

  (Art & design series)
  "Based upon Get me to the printer"
  "A Spectrum book."
  Includes index.
    1. Printing, Practical—Handbooks, manuals, etc.
  2. Graphic arts—Handbooks, manuals, etc.   3. Small
  business—Handbooks, manuals, etc.   4. Corporations, Non-
  profit—Handbooks, manuals, etc.   I. Frank, Susan.
  II. Levine, Mindy N., 1955—. Get me to the printer
  on time, on or under the budget, and looking good.
  III. Title.   IV. Series.
  Z244.3.L443   1984   686.2′24   84-7231
  ISBN 0-13-453960-5
  ISBN 0-13-453952-4 (pbk.)

Editorial/production supervision: Inkwell
Book design: Alice R. Mauro
Cover design: Hal Siegel
Manufacturing buyer: Ed Ellis
This book is available at a special discount when ordered
in bulk quantities. Contact Prentice-Hall, Inc.,
General Publishing Division, Special Sales,
Englewood Cliffs, N. J. 07632.
In Print: A Concise Guide to Graphic Arts and Printing
for Small Businesses and Nonprofit Organizations
by Mindy N. Levine with Susan Frank
© 1984 by Prentice-Hall, Inc., Englewood Cliffs, New Jersey 07632
Based upon Get Me to the Printer
Copyright © 1981 by Off-Off Broadway Alliance, Inc.
A Spectrum Book

10   9   8   7   6   5   4   3   2   1

Prentice-Hall International, Inc., *London*
Prentice-Hall of Australia Pty. Limited, *Sydney*
Prentice-Hall Canada Inc., *Toronto*
Prentice-Hall of India Private Limited, *New Delhi*
Prentice-Hall of Japan, Inc., *Tokyo*
Prentice-Hall of Southeast Asia Pte. Ltd., *Singapore*
Whitehall Books Limited, *Wellington, New Zealand*
Editora Prentice-Hall do Brasil Ltda., *Rio de Janeiro*

ISBN 0-13-453960-5

ISBN 0-13-453952-4 {PBK}

Special thanks to Nancy Heller
whose guidance and collaboration
helped make this book possible.

Contents

Foreword

The idea of this book, its initial research and funding, originated at the offices of the Alliance of Resident Theatres/New York (formerly known as the Off Off Broadway Alliance.) The Alliance provides essential marketing, management, and information services to theatre artists and administrators, related arts professionals, and audiences. A publication program on monographs and full-length books (on topics ranging from box office procedures to theatre renovation) is one component of the Alliance's diverse activities. This book grew out of the Alliance's continuing efforts to respond to the practical concerns of its members.

Recognizing the need to de-mystify the process of printing and graphics, Nancy Heller, former Alliance Executive Director, commissioned writer Mindy N. Levine and graphic designer Susan Frank to prepare a monograph that would address this problem in a clear, straightforward manner. *Get Me to the Printer,* published in 1981, resulted. Demand for the book was so great that its first printing sold out rapidly. It became clear that the book would be of interest to many persons outside the arts community. Working in conjunction with Prentice-Hall, a new publication was planned that would be useful to a wider audience.

Increasingly, projects initiated by the Alliance are serving a constituency far beyond the New York theatre community. We are indeed excited that *In Print* will benefit so many different associations and individuals throughout the country. To those who helped make the publication of this book possible—particularly Chemical Bank for their financial support to *Get Me to the Printer,* and the Alliance staff—we extend our special thanks.

Mark B. Simon
Administrative Director
Alliance of Resident Theatres/New York

Jane S. Moss
Executive Director
Alliance of Resident Theatres/New York

Preface

From the simplest typewritten press release to a complex four color brochure, the decisions you make concerning graphics will determine how effectively your message communicates. Good graphic design creates order from confusion. It finds an aesthetically pleasing, but not necessarily expensive way to organize material and achieve a certain goal. Most importantly, it speaks for you just as your services or product do. Used effectively, it can generate interest in your organization and help establish an identity for you within the public mind. In today's fiercely competitive market effective graphic design becomes an important tool in insuring the success of your endeavor—be it a theatrical performance, a new restaurant, a babysitting service, or a charity benefit.

To the uninitiated the graphic arts process can seem baffling and complex, for it makes use of many technical processes and draws on the skills of numerous craftsmen—designers, typesetters and printers. But it need not be mysterious. Armed with a working knowledge of how type is set, how copy is prepared and how a piece is printed, your organization can approach the graphic design and printing process with a minimum of difficulties. *In Print* is written for those organizations who work in conjunction with a graphic designer as well as those who prepare their own flyers, brochures and posters. The first edition of this book was created specifically with performing arts groups in mind. It has been revised and expanded so that the basic information contained in this book will be of use to any individual or organization who is responsible for producing printed material with efficient, economic and effective results.

IN
PRINT

S T E P

1

Developing

the Design

Design Preliminaries

The first step in creating printed material—be it a flyer, subscription brochure, or advertisement—has nothing to do with typesetting, printing, grades of paper, halftone screens, or any other technicalities involved in the process. The procedure begins with an assessment of your needs and resources. Before you contact a designer (or sit down to create your own piece), you must have a clear conception of what you wish your graphics to accomplish. A graphic designer can be of enormous help, for he/she can make aesthetic decisions about the most pleasing and effective way to arrange material for maximum legibility and clarity and can oversee your job from concept to finished piece. But a designer cannot tell you what you should say, nor how much money you can and should spend. Initiate the design and printing process by asking the following questions.

Copy Content

What information must be communicated? Determine what you want to say, whom you want to reach, and the image you wish to communicate about your organization. Type a draft of the information that will appear in your piece. This is known as "rough copy." It can be revised and refined at a later date but at this initial stage it is important to determine:

- Tone of copy—will it be serious or whimsical, academic or offbeat?
- Content of copy—will it include brief quotations, long descriptive paragraphs, a subscription blank?
- Approximate length of copy

Artwork and Photographs

What artwork or photographs are available or can be obtained? In selecting photographs, provide the designer with several, both vertical and horizontal, that are sharply focused, have good contrast and a full range of tones.

Budget

How much money is available? Be realistic. Remember that printing 1,000 copies of a mailer can cost as little as $30.00 for a photocopied, handwritten flyer or as much as several thousand dollars for a four color process brochure.

Timetable

What is your timetable? It is imperative that you start your project well in advance. Graphic design and printing are multi-step processes drawing on the skills and talents of many people. Mishaps can and do occur so allow sufficient lead time. By anticipating your needs you may be able to economize by gang printing, that is, printing several jobs on the same sheet of paper. For example, while printing a flyer you might also run a funding brochure, stationery, and box office forms; or run your job with that of another organization. The sheet is later cut into individual jobs and the price pro-rated.

Working with a Graphic Designer

Graphic design is a highly personal matter. What some individuals consider brilliant design others find unappealing. In hiring a graphic designer you are buying taste and technical expertise, saving yourself time and substantial worry, and perhaps ultimately saving money. Select an individual who has an aesthetic sensibility you admire, one with whom you feel comfortable working, who has the organizational ability to maintain your schedule and budget, and whose fee you can afford.

Choosing a Graphic Designer

Consult with other organizations like your own for suggestions concerning talented designers. They will no doubt be familiar with artists who are accustomed to and enjoy working with low budget organizations and understand the budgetary constraints involved. By maintaining a clipping file of interesting brochures and advertisements you can develop a useful reference source of good designers.

If time allows, make appointments with several designers and review their portfolios. Designers are accustomed to showing their work, and there is no charge for this preliminary review.

If you cannot afford to hire a professional designer, consider contacting a nearby university or art school.

Inexperienced designers will often work for a negligible fee in order to build a portfolio of printed material. Remember, however, that although these individuals may possess excellent design sense, they frequently lack experience dealing with typesetters, printers, and paper, and therefore may fail to make the most economical and expedient design choices.

If you decide to handle the job yourself, read this handbook carefully and remember to keep things simple. A complicated project such as a four-color process brochure probably should not be attempted without the assistance of a graphic designer. In dealing with printers and typesetters don't be afraid to ask questions. Try to work with craftsmen who care about your piece, even if it is a relatively small job.

First Meeting with the Graphic Designer: Communicating Your Ideas

At the first meeting with the graphic designer it is your responsibility to communicate as clearly and explicitly as possible how you envision your piece. Indicate the audience you wish to reach and the feeling you hope to engender. If you have a clipping file, it may prove useful in making points about your likes and dislikes. Provide the designer with rough copy and any photographs or artwork you think may be appropriate. Be certain to review budgetary limitations, but allow the designer to decide how the money will be allocated to the various components of the job——art, type, printing and paper. Establish a firm time schedule, working backward from the time you want finished pieces in your office or at a mailing house. Ascertain the designer's fee and clarify what services it includes. Designers generally charge a flat rate for design concept and follow-through work, and bill the preparation of the mechanical and the cost of photostats, typesetting and printing separately. If you are willing to assume the added responsibility of obtaining estimates, negotiating with typesetters and printers and overseeing production, ask the designer

if you can be billed directly for printing and typesetting costs. This will save you the mark-up that
designers customarily take on contracted services, but will necessitate that you make a greater
commitment of time to the project.

The designer's principal responsibility at the
first meeting is to listen and develop a firm under-
standing of your needs. He/she will then prepare
two or three rough sketches of possible design
solutions.

Second Meeting with the Graphic Designer: The Rough Sketch or "Comp"

Based on your preliminary meeting, the designer
will prepare several visualizations of possible design solutions. Drawn to scale, these will enable
you to picture the look of your final piece. The relative placement of art and type will be indicated.
Type will be rendered with a series of straight or
curved lines with one or two words written out in
full to suggest type size and style. If color is to be
used, this will be shown on the comp.

When reviewing the comp:

- Speak openly about your feelings. You
  may like one sketch immediately, or the
  type style of one and the color of another.
  Frequently, design elements of various
  sketches can be combined.

Eight page folder
using French fold

Panel 1

Panel 2

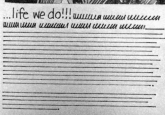

Panel 3

Panels 4-7

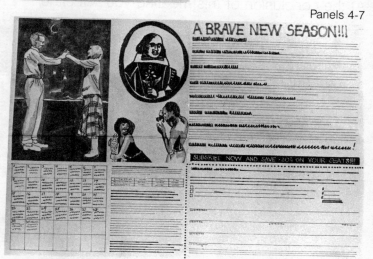

Panel 8 is back of brochure

- Make certain the proper relative importance has been given to all elements. The design may be beautiful, but if the title of your organization is hidden in the corner, the piece won't succeed in achieving your objective.
- Confirm that there is sufficient room for all the copy you plan to include.
- If the piece is to be mailed, check that it conforms with postal regulations (see Appendix II); if it is an advertisement, make certain your designer is aware of where it is to be placed and that publication's design specifications and restrictions (see Appendix I).

At the conclusion of this meeting you will either:

- Give the designer approval to proceed.
- Request that the designer make certain changes and then proceed.
- Ask the designer to prepare additional comps for your review.

Preparing
Your Own
Rough Sketch

I f you are working without the assistance of a graphic designer you should, after assessing your needs and defining your budget and time schedule, begin experimenting with visual ideas. A rough sketch is like a sophisticated doodle. Let your imagination run free and trust your design sense. However, remember that clarity and readability are of the utmost importance and consider the following elements.

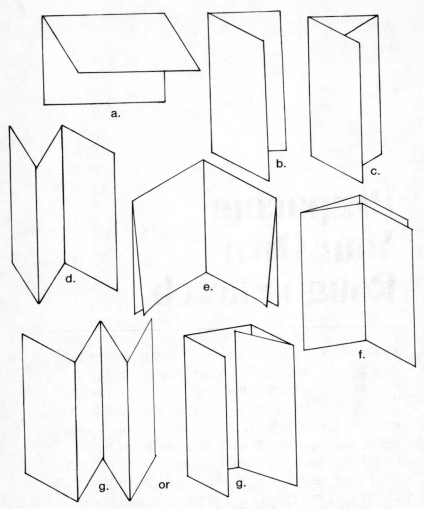

Four page folder: one fold along either the (a) short or (b) long dimension

Six page folder: made with two parallel folds, either (c) regular or (d) accordion

Eight page folder: with (e) French fold—one parallel and one right angle fold (f) two parallel folds and (g) three parallel accordion folds

Size

It is advisable to choose standard sizes. Odd size pages can lead to paper waste and significantly increase the cost of your project. Discuss size considerations with your printer. Certain presses have size limitations or are particularly suited for handling specific jobs. Make sure your piece conforms with postal regulations (see Appendix II).

Folding

Folding allows for the isolation and organization of material in different quadrants. Cut a sheet of paper to the size of your piece and experiment with various folding methods. Several possibilities are pictured on page 14.

Type Size & Weight

A type sample book that shows various type styles and sizes can be obtained free of cost from a local typesetter. Try not to use type that is smaller than 10 points except for photo credits, disclaimers, and coupons (see page 44 for a discussion of point size). If you plan to use reverses (white type on a dark ground), do not use type that is smaller than 12 points, and avoid thin type faces as they are very difficult to read.

Artwork

If you do not have photographs or illustrations that are appropriate for your piece, it may still be possible to incorporate visual materials. There are numerous sources where interesting graphics and photographs can be obtained.

New York Public Library Picture Collections: Many libraries maintain extensive clipping files of artwork and illustrations from old books and magazines. Arranged by subject matter, the material is in the public domain and available free of charge.

Dover Publications: Dover Publications issues a series of books containing art on numerous subjects. Prepared specifically to meet the needs of graphic designers, these books can be purchased at most art stores. Volumes in the series range from art nouveau decorative borders to bold geometric shapes, from floral patterns to astrological symbols. Average price for these publications is $3.50.

Commercial Picture Archives: Several picture archives sell artwork to meet graphic needs of designers. Their fees are based on use, so for as little as $75.00–$100.00 your organization can obtain artwork that would cost an advertising agency a substantial fee.

Samples of visual material:
line art that may be used
instead of photographs.

Postal Regulations

Be certain your piece conforms with postal regulations. Regulations for 3rd class mailing pieces stipulate that cards or folders be no larger than 11½" × 13½" or no smaller than 3½" × 5", weigh less than 2.8 ounces and be thinner than ¼". Mailers should leave at least 3½ inches from the top and 3½ inches from the right clear space for address information. Mailers larger than letter size must leave 3 inches from the top and 4¼ inches from the right clear space. The address, logo and indicia must be parallel to the flyer's length and the closed fold must be on the top.

Using Color

 olor can bring clarity, flexibility, and complexity to design. It can be used to attract attention and make a piece more competitive with sophisticated advertising. But the mere introduction of color makes a piece neither successful nor high-quality. It must be incorporated as an integrated and appropriate element of the design. With the addition of each new color there is a corresponding (but not strictly proportional) increase in price. However, one or two colors properly used can yield a full range of design possibilities. Two basic processes are involved in color reproduction: Flat (or match) color and four color process.

Flat Color

Flat color is used when a piece contains no color photographs. Most flat color jobs use from one to four colors with two being the most common.

One Color Jobs

As the name indicates, a one color job is printed with one color. This is frequently misconstrued to mean a black and white job. However, one color refers to the ink, which may be any color—blue, red, green, purple, black. As the color of the paper is not counted as a color, this allows for diverse possibilities—red ink on yellow paper, brown ink on blue paper, black ink on green paper, etc. Brilliantly colored paper stock or ink

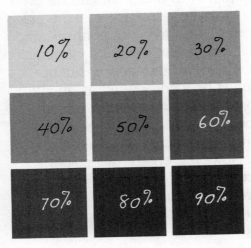

Benday Screens

should be avoided for the printing of logo, indicia, and address, as they may be rejected by the post office.

Further flexibility can be achieved through screening. A *Benday Screen* can introduce tonalities within a piece. Type may be printed solid at 100% value or screened to produce tints from 5% to 95%. For example, a screen thrown over red ink at 50% will bring pink into the design. Thus one could use both red and pink for type. Alternatively, type can be reversed. The ink color is used to cover everything but the type, which appears as the color of the paper. The inked background can then be screened to achieve additional tonalities.

When screening and/or reversing type, keep type sufficiently large and bold to remain legible. Light color type should be avoided, as it is difficult and uncomfortable to read. Readability is likewise impaired when black type is used against deep, dark colors.

Two Color Jobs

A two color job significantly multiplies design possibilities. Not only can the two colors be used separately, but they can be screened and combined to yield a full range of colors. Two color jobs are usually printed with black as the second color (again, the color of the paper does not count as a color). This permits the text and halftones to be printed in black. The second color can be used decoratively, or to create headlines. For example, by using black and red ink on white paper one can print black type on red, pink, or white; red type on grey, pink, or white; grey type on white, pink, or red; and white type on black, grey, or red; as well as using the colors and their tints as design elements.

Three and Four Color Jobs

The techniques of three and four color jobs resemble those of two color jobs. The design possibilities are simply multiplied. Most jobs are designed as one, two, or four color jobs. To do a three color job a printer usually uses a four color press, so the price differential between a three and four color job is negligible. Some neighborhood printers will run a piece several times on a one color press to produce two, three, and four color jobs.

For a price comparison of one, two, three, and four color jobs, see Appendix III.

Specifying Flat Color

Color is specified to the printer by choosing a color from the *Pantone Matching System* (PMS), a standardized system of over 500 colors. The colors are numbered and arranged in swatch

PANTONE	PANTONE	PANTONE	PANTONE	PANTONE	PANTONE
434	434	434	434	434	434

PANTONE	PANTONE	PANTONE	PANTONE	PANTONE	PANTONE
435	435	435	435	435	435

PANTONE	PANTONE	PANTONE	PANTONE	PANTONE	PANTONE
436	436	436	436	436	436

PANTONE	PANTONE	PANTONE	PANTONE	PANTONE	PANTONE
437	437	437	437	437	437

PANTONE	PANTONE	PANTONE	PANTONE	PANTONE	PANTONE
438	438	438	438	438	438

PANTONE	PANTONE	PANTONE	PANTONE	PANTONE	PANTONE
439	439	439	439	439	439

PANTONE	PANTONE	PANTONE	PANTONE	PANTONE	PANTONE
440	440	440	440	440	440

Sample page from PMS swatch book that shows tones of grey.

books that can be purchased at any art supply shop. The number of the desired color is indicated to the printer. Swatch books show colors printed on both coated and uncoated paper (see page 29 for a discussion of paper). The color of the paper will also affect the appearance of any color that is printed on it. Swatch books are printed on white stock, but books that show color inks printed on color paper are available, mostly through paper companies.

Four Color Process

Four color process is used to reproduce the full color spectrum. It is frequently confused with four color flat printing, but they are very different processes. Four color flat printing uses any four ink colors, while four color process makes use of four specific colors—process yellow, magenta (process red), cyan (process blue), and process black.

Color in four color process is not created by a mixing of inks. Instead, the four colors are printed as a series of dots which the eye optically mixes to yield the full range of colors in the original image, much as it does when watching a color television set or viewing a pointillist painting.

Color Separations

To reproduce full color artwork, it is necessary to break down the original into four separate colors. This is done by photographing and screening the original four times through different filters. Photographing through a red filter produces a negative record of red light; a positive of this negative will contain everything but red——that is, blue and green or cyan. Photographing through a green filter produces a color separation to appear in red; photographing through a violet filter produces the separation film to appear in yellow; photographing through an orange/red filter produces the separation to appear in cyan and photographing the same photograph through a yellow filter produces a separation filter that will print in process black.

As each filter covers one third of the spectrum when the positives are combined and printed, all the colors of the original should be reproduced. However, because of the impurities in ink pigments the true colors do not reproduce precisely. Color usually appears muddied and corrections must be made on the separation negatives.

The printer will supply you with progressive proofs, series of proofs showing each color printed alone and in sequential combination with other colors. Color emphasis can be changed by marking instructions to the printer—"too red," "too blue," and so forth.

Because of the time and expense involved, many organizations find it impractical to use four color process, particularly since so many interesting and inventive effects can be achieved with one and two colors. If you decide to use four color process, make sure you allow sufficient time for printing. Although technological innovations have significantly speeded the separation process, creating and correcting color separations can still take as long as ten working days. Prep and press time is quite costly.

Choosing Paper

A choice of paper should be made as early as possible in the design process. For the past several years there has been a paper shortage, so paper is no longer heavily stockpiled. Provide the printer with as much lead time as possible so he/she can order your paper in advance. The primary characteristics to be concerned with when choosing a paper are its weight, opacity, and finish. Your aesthetic preferences, the requirements of the job, and economic factors will influence your choice.

Weight

Known as basis weight, the weight of a paper is calibrated as the weight in pounds of 500 sheets of standard paper for that grade. The standard size of bond paper is approximately 17″ × 22″, newsprint is approximately 24″ × 36″, book paper is approximately 25″ × 38″, and cover stock is approximately 20″ × 26″. "Basis 80" means that 500 sheets of 25″ × 38″ book weight paper weighs 80 pounds. Brochures are usually printed on 60, 70, or 80 pound text weight stock, a type of book paper.

Choose a weight that is neither so light that it feels flimsy, nor so heavy that it feels cumbersome and will add extra postage to your mailing. Remember that 3rd class mailing pieces must weigh less than 2.8 ounces and be less than ¼ inch thick. Lighter weight papers may be appropriate for pieces that fold, since the folding process causes paper to "bulk-up," giving it a heavier feel.

Opacity

Opacity refers to the capacity of a paper to take ink on one side without showing through on the other side. This is extremely important if you plan to print on both sides. Paper must be sufficiently opaque so that the reader will not be distracted by print showing through from the other side.

Finish

Finish refers to the surface treatment of paper. Paper comes both coated and uncoated.

Uncoated paper is recommended for jobs that are all text, including postcards and invitations. It ranges from inexpensive newsprint to the finest parchment. Popular uncoated book papers include antique, eggshell, and machine finish. Uncoated paper allows you to achieve greater bulk with less weight.

Coated Paper has a special coating that gives it a slick finish. The coating buries fibers so they do not come into contact with printing ink. Rather than being absorbed into the paper, the ink rests on the paper's surface, yielding a more brilliant image. Coated papers may have dull or glossy finishes. The higher the gloss, the more brilliant the reproduction of photographs or color. High gloss paper is not recommended for jobs with extensive line copy, as its reflective surface makes reading difficult.

In choosing a paper ask your designer or printer for a dummy, a sample of paper cut to the size of your piece. Fold it, hold it by the corner to see if it's too flimsy, write on it to test its opacity, and determine if you like the way it feels. If your piece is a mailer that requires a return response, write on it to confirm that ink markings will not smudge.

STEP

2

Obtaining

Printing Estimates

Preparing
for Presstime

O nce a design has been developed and approved, printing estimates should be solicited. This should be done well in advance so the printer has time to order paper and reserve press time. Don't wait until *you're* ready to go to press before you begin to think about printing.

Liaison with the printer is usually the responsibility of the graphic designer. If you are handling the job yourself, call several printers for estimates on your job (get suggestions of good printers from your colleagues). Corporations that have their own print shops may be willing to contribute printing as an in-kind service to not-for-profit companies. You must provide the printer with the following specifications:

- Quantity
- Number of colors
- Type of paper*
- Weight of paper*
- Size of piece
- Size of piece when folded down
- Number of folds
- Number of halftones
- Size of halftones
- Bleeds**
- To print on one or two sides
- Schedule

When the printer quotes you on a job, ask for a written estimate. This will facilitate comparisons between various printers and help avoid confusion and misunderstanding at a later date. Don't assume that a price is absolute. If the printer you most want to work with has not given

---

* If you are unfamiliar with paper, explain your needs to the printer. He will suggest an appropriate paper for the job.

** Bleed refers to the area of print or plate that extends beyond the edge of the page, rather than being enclosed, and applies mostly to color or photographs. A printer must use a slightly larger sheet to accommodate bleeds.

you the lowest bid, ask if a price adjustment is possible.

Printers usually print and charge you for overages—an excess of the quantity you actually ordered. Although this is an accepted trade custom, adopted to allow for waste inherent in the printing process, you may wish to inquire if it is possible to exclude overages from the price. However, estimate the quantity you require carefully. The principal cost of printing a job is the make-ready—that is, setting up the press for printing—which remains constant, no matter how many copies you print. Therefore, the larger the run, the lower the cost per piece. It is safer and more economical to print slightly more than you need than to be forced to go back to press a second time because you underestimated quantity. For a chart comparing the variable cost of a brochure based on quantity, the number of colors, and weight of paper, see Appendix III.

STEP

3

Preproduction:

Typesetting

Introduction

During preproduction all copy must be prepared so it can be assembled to create a mechanical—a paste-up of all type, photos, and line art—from which the printer will make a plate for printing. If you are working with a designer, your major responsibility during this phase will be to prepare finished copy and proofread it carefully when it is returned from the typesetter.

If you are preparing your own piece, it will be necessary to become familiar with typographic terminology and processes.

Preparing
Final Copy

Final copy is the exact text that will appear on your printed material including descriptive copy, quotes, and photo captions. It should be typed, double spaced, on a sheet of 8½"
× 11" white bond. Use wide margins so there is ample room to indicate instructions to the typesetter. (See page 53 on specifying type.) Use only one side of the page and number all pages. Identify each sheet at the top to avoid mix-ups. *Proofread your copy several times and have at least one other person proofread it. Careful checking of copy at this stage is essential!* Even if the typesetter suspects there is an error, he/she will set it just as it is written. Any mistakes will be

costly in terms of time and money. Making corrections once copy has been set can often be as expensive as setting the original job, since typesetting is charged at an hourly rate and it is time consuming to put your job back on the machine, search out the errors, and make the necessary corrections.

Double check that your copy contains all pertinent information. For example, if you are advertising a special event—theatre program, lecture, community board meeting, New Year's Eve gala, or charity benefit—the following data should appear:

- Title of program
- Name of sponsoring group
- Date of event
- Time of event
- Place and address of event
- Ticket information including discounts
- Phone number for reservations and information; subscription coupon if applicable
- Descriptive or selling copy including pertinent quotes
- Special credits (photo, funding, and design)
- Indicia
- Return address

Typographic Terminology

Before delivering final copy to the typesetter it must be marked so he/she knows exactly how it is to be set. Clear indications should be given concerning type size, line length, spacing between lines, type style, and line arrangement. A working knowledge of basic type characteristics and typographic terminology is necessary for accurate communication with the typesetter.

Type Size

Type is measured in *points*. A point measures
.0138 inches or approximately $1/72$ of an inch.
The most popular typefaces range from 6 points
to 72 points. Typefaces 14 points and smaller
are called *text types;* those larger than 14 points
are called *display types*. Point sizes are illustrated
on page 45.

Line Length

The length of a line is measured in picas. There
are twelve points to one pica or six picas to an
inch. The line you are reading is 21 picas long.

Spacing

The amount of spacing between lines is known as
leading (pronounced ledding) or *linespacing* and
is measured in points. Aesthetics, readability, and
space considerations influence decisions concerning leading. If ten point type is set with one
point leading it is set as ''10 on 11'' and is specified as 10/11. The first numeral, 10,
designates the type size; the second figure indicates the size of the character plus leading.

All the world's a stage

6 Point — All the world's a stage

8 Point — All the world's a stage

10 Point — All the world's a stage

14 Point — All the world's a stage

24 Point — All the world's a stage

48 Point — All the world's a stage

72 Point — All the world's a

And all the men and women merely players:
They have their exits and their entrances;   9/9

And all the men and women merely players:
They have their exits and their entrances;   9/10

And all the men and women merely players:
They have their exits and their entrances;   9/11

GARAMOND

All the world's a stage	(No. 3)
All the world's a stage	(No. 3 Italic)
All the world's a stage	(No. 3 Bold)
All the world's a stage	(No. 3 Bold Italic)
All the world's a stage	(Ultra Bold Condensed)

HELVETICA

All the world's a stage	(Light)
All the world's a stage	(Regular)
All the world's a stage	(Italic)
All the world's a stage	(Medium)
All the world's a stage	(Heavy)

SERIF GOTHIC

All the world's a stage	(Light)
All the world's a stage	(Regular)
All the world's a stage	(Bold)
All the world's a stage	(Heavy)
All the world's a stage	(Black)

Type Styles

There are hundreds of styles of type ranging from script to print, fine to heavy line, old fashioned to contemporary. Ask your typesetter to supply you with a type book. This will allow you to visualize what type styles look like in various point sizes. Some of the more popular type styles include Helvetica, Garamond, and Times Roman.

Type Families

Some type styles have many variations—light face, medium, extra bold, expanded, and condensed. Known as *type families*, these variations allow the designer great flexibility while preserving a unity of design. They are particularly useful in designing pieces where there is often a need to differentiate between quotes, headlines, and descriptive copy.

Line Arrangement

Type can be arranged in five basic ways.
Justified—lines are the same length and align on both the left and right
Unjustified flush left—lines of different lengths align on the left and are ragged on the right
Unjustified flush right—lines of different lengths align on the right and are ragged on the left

A l l t h e w o r l d ' s a s t a g e , And all the men and women merely players:	Justified
All the world's a stage, And all the men and women merely players:	Unjustified flush left
All the world's a stage, And all the men and women merely players:	Unjustified flush right
All the world's a stage, And all the men and women merely players:	Centered
All the world's a stage, And all the men and women merely players:	Random

Centered—lines of unequal lengths align by their center points along a vertical spine, with both sides ragged

Random—lines are arranged with no discernible pattern

Wordspacing and Letterspacing

The amount of spacing between words and letters is frequently adjusted for readability, aesthetics, or to fill a certain area. Corrective wordspacing and letterspacing are used when margins are justified.

Copyfitting

Deciding on what point size and leading to use is more than an aesthetic choice. Copy to be set must fit properly in the space that has been allocated for it in the design. If you chose a point size that is too small, unwanted space will be generated and the aesthetic impact of the design will be undermined. If you use type that is too large, not all the copy will fit in the available space. Copyfitting is accomplished through a series of simple mathematical calculations and ratios. If you know how many characters are in your copy and how many characters of a specific typeface fit into a particular width, you can calculate how many lines there will be when copy is set. To insure that copy "fits" follow the steps enumerated below:

1. Determine what style type you wish to use. Not all typefaces of the same point size take up the same amount of space.

2. Calculate the number of characters in your copy by counting the number of characters (including spaces between words) in an average line and multiplying the number of characters per line by the number of lines.

3. Measure, in picas, the width of space into which you wish to insert your copy. This can be accomplished by measuring the space with a ruler and then converting inches to picas (1 inch equals 6 picas), or more easily, by using a pica rule, a ruler calibrated in picas and available at any art supply shop.

4. Determine how many characters of the typeface you wish to use fit in your specified width. This is done by consulting a chart in a type book.

5. Calculate how many lines there will be by dividing the total number of characters in your copy (Step 2) by the number of characters in a given width (Step 4).

6. Determine how long your copy depth will fall by consulting a Haberule, a specially calibrated ruler (available at art supply shops) that shows how long a specific number of lines (Step 5) in a particular point size will measure.

7. If copy falls too long, you must choose a smaller type size. If it falls too short, you can choose a larger point size or add more leading between lines.

Specifying Type

ypesetting instructions are given to the typesetter by writing indications on the typed manuscript concerning size, leading, typeface, measure, and margins, in that order. A complete specification might read as "10/12 Times Roman x 20 justified," which means "set in 10 point Times Roman type with a 2 point leading between lines in a column that is 20 picas wide with lines of equal length that align on the left and the right."

In addition to type specifications, indicate whether paragraphs should be indented or kept flush left. Mark headings flush left, flush right, centered or indented, according to design.

Keep in mind that underlining a word has a very specific meaning for a typesetter (see page 68 for proofing marks). One underline means set in italic, two means set in small caps, and three means set in all caps. A wavy line means set in bold face.

Check your work carefully, making certain that all your instructions are clear. Remember, the person setting your copy has no familiarity with how it will ultimately be incorporated into your design.

Choosing a Typesetting System

Decisions concerning typesetting methods and typographic style will strongly influence the appearance of your piece. Many characteristics—formality, informality, delicacy, strength—can be suggested by the typeface used. The "right" typesetting system for your job is not necessarily the one that produces the highest quality typography. Often speed and cost are important factors to be considered.

Personal Calligraphy

This is the simplest and least expensive way to render copy. All that is needed is a pen and a steady hand. Used with care, it can give your piece a highly individualistic, innovative character. Frequently, however, it may appear sloppy and amateurish.

Calligraphy is not recommended when extensive copy must be set.

Transfer Type

For a low budget job with a small amount of copy, transfer type is an ideal method. Frequently referred to by the brand names Letraset or Prestype, it can be purchased at any art supply shop. The type, which comes in numerous typefaces and sizes, is carried on sheets approximately 10″ × 14″ and is applied manually, letter by letter. See page 36 for an explanation of how to use transfer type.

Typewriter

For a low budget job, simply typing your material may be appropriate. Use a typewriter that produces sharp, uniform letters—preferably one with a carbon film ribbon. The type in this book was set with a typewriter. By combining this method with transfer type, perhaps adding bold headlines and ornamental borders, a striking graphic statement can be achieved with minimal expenditure. Type may be enlarged or reduced through photostating (see page 77), further extending the flexibility of this method.

Strike-On Composition

Basically a sophisticated typewriting system, strike-on composition offers a greater range of typefaces and sizes and has the capacity to justify margins. However, like typewriting, the system cannot set large display headlines. This method is sometimes referred to as "cold type."

Handset Composition

Handset composition is produced by assembling individual metal characters into a composing stick, much as Gutenberg did in 1450. A slow, antiquated method of setting type, it occasionally is used to set tickets.

Hot Type

This method involves casting type from molten metal and is therefore known as hot type. The four major processes—Linotype, Intertype, Monotype and Ludlow—generate slugs or matrices with raised letter surfaces. These are then inked to produce letter impressions. Once the most popular method of setting type, hot type has been superseded by phototypesetting. However, many small printers who also maintain their own typesetting shops continue to use hot type.

Phototypesetting

Also known as photocomposing, phototypesetting provides a fast, flexible, relatively inexpensive method of setting type. In phototypesetting letters are projected onto photosensitive paper or film. This results in a much sharper letter image than machine composition where the edges of the letterform are sometimes irregular due to variable ink distribution.

There is a tremendous range in quality and sophistication among typesetting systems, but all of them contain a keyboard system and photounit that includes a master character image, a light source, and a photo or light sensitive material.

Before copy is set it is typed into a keyboard that resembles a typewriter with additional special function keys for typeface, leading, letterspacing, and so forth. Most units then produce either a perforated tape, a magnetic tape, or a magnetic disc that is used to drive the photounit. Economy models set type directly without storing it.

There are two basic keyboard systems, counting and noncounting. In a counting system, also known as input justified, the operator makes all end of the line decisions concerning hyphenation, justification of margins, and adjustment of wordspacing. In noncounting keyboard systems, the operator produces an unjustified or "idiot" tape that is then justified by computer. The advantage of this system is speed and simplicity. The disadvantage is that in less sophisticated, nonhyphenating computer programs, irregular and distracting wordspacing may be produced. If copy must be set on a hyphenless system, consider setting it flush left, ragged right, as this copy is set. This will allow for even wordspacing and any excess space will be less noticeable at the end of the line.

Once copy has been keyboarded, the type or disc is fed into the photounit, triggering the selection of characters from a master character set. A high intensity light is flashed through the character and the beam is subsequently deflected by mirrors and prisms and projected onto photosensitive paper or film. In many systems, lenses can reduce or enlarge point size.

Many neighborhood copy shops are beginning to incorporate typesetting equipment (usually phototypesetting) into their facilities so they can offer a full range of reproductive services. The convenience of these operations should be weighed against their cost and quality. It is a good idea to make price comparisons with full service typesetting shops.

Correcting Reader's Proofs

Once type has been set, the typographer will send you a *reader's proof* (also known as a *galley proof,* or rough proof) so you can check that copy has been set correctly. Read the proof carefully several times and have at least one other person read it. Mark all corrections in the margin with a colored pen using standard proofreading marks (see chart on page 63). All corrections should be marked either *PE* or *AA*. *PE* stands for printer's error and these will be corrected free of charge. *AA* stands for *author's alteration* and refers to any corrections you or the designer make that were not on your final copy. These changes will be billed additionally, usually at an hourly rate of at least $35.00. Author's Alterations are costly and time consuming. They can be minimized by proofing your final copy with great care.

When you are certain you have caught all errors, send the proofs back to the typesetter. He/she will make corrections and then produce *reproduction proofs* or *repros*. These will be used by the designer to create a mechanical, a paste-up of all artwork and type that will be delivered to the printer.

You will still be able to make corrections later, when you check the mechanical and when you review the blueprint. However, every effort should be made to avoid changes after this point. The later in the process you make alterations, the more costly they become.

Proofreading Marks

Insert comma	⌄	Transpose (th*er*, only is)	*tr*	
Insert apostrophe	⌄	Align	=	
Insert quotation marks	⌄⌄	Insert space	#	
Insert period	⊙	Hair space between letters	*hr #*	
Insert colon	⊙	Push down space	⊔	
Insert semicolon	;/	Move to left	⊏	
Insert question mark	?/	Move to right	⊐	
Insert hyphen	=/	Lower	⊔	
One-em dash	⊥	Elevate	⊓	
Two-em dash	⅔ⅿ	Broken letter	X	
En dash	*en*	Spell out (U.S)	🆂🅿	
Ellipsis	.̣.̣.̣.̣	Let it stand (some day)	*stet*	
Delete	⌿	Wrong font	*wf*	
Close up	⌒	Set in boldface type	*bf*	
Delete and close up	⌒	Set in roman type	*rom*	
Reverse; upside-down	9	Set in italic type	*ital*	
Insert (caret)	∧	Small capitals	*sc*	
Paragraph	¶	Capitals	*caps*	
No paragraph; run in	no ¶	Set in lower case	*lc*	
		Insert lead between lines	*/d⟩*	

Original
manuscript,
Showing mark-up,
Sent to printer.

Seven Ages of Man *Caps*

WILLIAM SHAKESPEARE *lc*
3 extra points

SET IN 18/20
GARAMOND #3,
Flush left

All the worlds a stage

and all the men and women merely players:

They have thier exits and their entrances;/

plays
And one man in his time/many parts

His acts being (7) ages. (sp)

Reader's proof
Showing mark-up
sent back
to printer.

SEVEN AGES OF MAN bf (AA)
William Shakespeare
#
All the world's a stage,] (AA)
                                                    —women (PE)
And all the men and (woman) merely players:
They have their exits and their entrances;
And one man in his time plays many parts (AA)
His acts being seven ages.

SEVEN AGES OF MAN
William Shakespeare

All the world's a stage,
And all the men and women merely players:
They have their exits and their entrances;
And one man in his time plays many parts,
His acts being seven ages.

Preproduction:

Artwork

Screening
Halftones

There are two different types of copy
that are assembled on a mechanical—*line copy* and *continuous tone
copy. Line copy* is any image that is
made up of solid black with no gradation of tone. It includes type, line diagrams,
and pen and ink drawings and is shot with high
contrast film that records just two tones—black
or white. *Continuous tone copy* is any image that
has a gradation of tones including photographs
and charcoal illustrations. Most printing processes
can reproduce only solid tones from a single
color ink. For example, when printing with black
ink, middle tones such as greys cannot be reproduced. Therefore, continuous tone copy must be

65 Line Screen

110 Line Screen

150 Line Screen

converted to line copy in order for it to be printed.
This is done by photographing copy through a
device known as a halftone screen that converts
continuous tone copy into a series of minute dots.
If you look at a photograph in a magazine or
newspaper under a magnifying glass you will note
that it is made of thousands of tiny dots. Because
of the limited resolving power of the human eye

the dots, or halftones, create an optical illusion
and appear to be continuous tone copy.

Screens come in a variety of coarsenesses as
well as patterns and are measured by the number
of "lines per inch"—which is the same as saying
"dots per inch." The more lines per inch, the
finer the dot pattern and the better the quality of
the halftone reproduction. Grade of paper, quality
of ink, and method of printing determine the type
of screen used. For example, newspapers require
coarse screens (65 for the *New York Times*, 85
for the *Village Voice*) while magazines, which use
smoother papers, are able to use finer screens
(up to 150 line) and thus obtain higher quality
photographs.

It is important to remember that screened art
cannot be rescreened. If you take a photograph
from a book (which has already been screened)
and rescreen it, a *moire* will be created. That is,
a distracting pattern of dots will be generated due
to the superimposition of a second screen.

Scaling Art

Before a mechanical can be made, photographs or artwork may need to be enlarged or reduced to fit within the design. Scaling changes the size of a piece of artwork without altering its relative dimensions. This can be achieved in two ways: the diagonal line or the proportional scale.

Diagonal Line

Place tracing paper over the artwork and draw a rectangle around it. Draw a diagonal line from the lower left corner through the upper right corner.

Diagonal Line Scaling

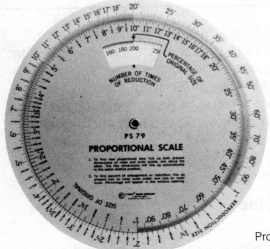

Proportional Scale

From the left corner measure off the new, enlarged or reduced width along the bottom of the rectangle. From this point draw a vertical line upward until it intersects the diagonal. The point of intersection represents the new height.

Proportional Scale

A proportional scale is a ratio wheel and can be obtained at any art supply shop. By aligning the desired width with the existing width on the ratio wheel, the height appears aligned with the old height. The proportional scale shows the percentage of enlargement and reduction. This figure is used when ordering photostats (see page 74) and when marking the mechanical for the printer.

Photostating

Photostats are inexpensive, high contrast photographic prints used to enlarge and reduce copy. Once you have determined through scaling how much you wish to enlarge or reduce your copy, take it to a photostat house. "Stat" houses can be found in any neighborhood of the city and are listed in the yellow pages under "Photocopying."

Photostats of continuous tone copy (photographs and charcoal illustrations) are not of sufficient quality to be used by the printer in preparing your piece. They are used to show size and position only and must be so marked when they are pasted onto the mechanical. The printer

Hattie Winston and Avery Brooks in Ntozake Shange's
A PHOTOGRAPH directed by Oz Scott. Photo by
Frederic Ohringer, courtesy of Joseph Papp,
Producer, New York Shakespeare Festival.

All the world's a stage
Positive

All the world's a stage
Negative

uses this as a guide when he "shoots"—or converts—the original artwork to halftone copy.

A special screened print of a continuous tone
copy, known as a *velox,* can be pasted into a
mechanical and shot with other line copy. To
make a velox, continuous tone copy must be
photographed through a halftone screen, trans-

78

forming the image into line copy by creating a series of dots. From this negative, a photoprint or velox is made. Making veloxes permits the designer to see the job with halftones in place, just as they will be when the job is printed, and saves the expense of having the printer strip in halftones. However, it diminishes the quality of halftone reproduction.

Veloxes must be used when preparing advertisements because newspapers and magazines will not strip in halftone negatives. It is essential to check a publication's screen requirements as veloxes are available in a wide range of screens —55, 60, 65, 85, 100, 110, and 120.

Photostats of line copy (type and illustrations) tend to polarize all tones to either black or white. These reproductions are high quality and unlike photostats of continuous tone copy can be pasted directly into the mechanical as original art.

Photostats can be either positive or negative. A positive stat looks just like the original. In a *negative stat* the values are reversed. For example, black type on a white background would print as white type on a black background. Some photostat houses must create a negative stat to generate a positive stat. With new technology "direct positives," also known as Photo Mechanical Transfers (PMT's) can be made.

If type has been specified and set incorrectly —either too large or too small—a photostatic enlargement or reduction can compensate inexpensively for the error.

Improving Photographic Quality/ Special Effects

Every effort should be made to obtain clearly focused, well balanced, and interesting artwork, for the higher the quality of original artwork, the finer the quality of reproduction. However, sometimes it is necessary to use inferior quality artwork. In such cases there are several screening and photostating techniques that a designer can use to overcome poor quality art and create special effects.

Silhouette

Silhouette

A halftone showing only selected areas. The printer removes all the halftone dots from the background by opaquing the negative with paint or by covering it with a mask.

Tinted Halftone

A black and white halftone that is screened and then printed over a flat background tint of another color.

Tinted Halftone

Halftone art converted to line art

Line Conversion

Continuous tone copy is converted to line copy through photostating or special effects photography, polarizing all tones to black or white. The photograph is then used for its geometric design,

Special Effects—White transfer type (lines) placed over line art

rather than its representational qualities and can
be printed over other colors. Screens may be
added to create special effects including wavy
lines, straight lines, cross-hatching, woodgrain,
and mezzotint. Line conversions can also be
created through the use of transfer type.

Screened halftone—Art greatly enlarged

Duotone

A two color halftone made from a black and white photograph. The photograph is shot twice, once for the black plate and once for the color plate. The black plate is shot for contrast to hold the dark tones and the color plate is shot for the middle tones. When printed the two plates produce a complete range of tones and the photograph obtains more depth and density.

STEP

5

Mechanicals

Introduction

 mechanical is the master from which a printing plate is made in order to print your piece. It contains all design elements—repros of type and photostats of art—pasted in position on a piece of illustration board, a smooth surfaced white cardboard. Photographs, which are treated separately by the printer, are not pasted onto the mechanical unless veloxes have been made.

Building Mechanicals

In order to make
a mechanical
you will need
the following materials:

- Drawing board with a metal edge
- Repros of type, or transfer type
- Photostats of illustrations or photographs
- T square
- Illustration board
- Masking tape
- Rubber cement
- Cement thinner

- Scissors
- Pointed tweezers
- Single edge razor blades or Exacto-knife
- Non-reproducing blue pencil
- Triangle

To begin, take the illustration board and square it up with your T square so it has 90° angles. Then, tape it securely to a drafting table or drawing board.

Drawing Guidelines

Using a T square, triangle, and non-reproducing blue pencil, draw the outside dimensions of the printing area, allowing a margin of a few inches all around for making notations to the printer. Light blue lines are not reproduced by the printing process so they may be drawn in freely.

Indicate the position of type and art with blue lines. These will serve as guidelines when pasting down art and ruling in boxes.

Crop Marks

Outside the printing area, in all four corners of the mechanical, mark the perimeter of the piece with a black pen. This will indicate to the printer where to trim the piece in order to make it the correct size.

Folding Lines

Indicate where the piece is to be folded with a black, broken line outside the trim area.

Holding Lines

With a red pen, outline the exact area that is to be occupied by a halftone or color tint.

Pasting Down Line Copy

Examine reproduction proofs carefully, checking to see that the typesetter has made all corrections

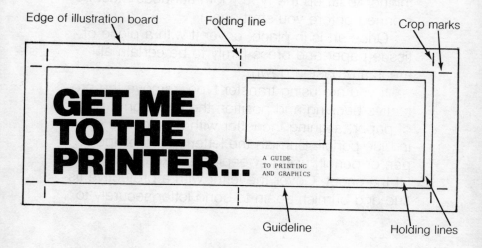

Edge of illustration board   Folding line   Crop marks

GET ME TO THE PRINTER...

A GUIDE
TO PRINTING
AND GRAPHICS

Guideline   Holding lines

requested and that the repros are clean and neat with no imperfections. Repros should be handled with the utmost care. Their quality will strongly influence the look of your final piece. If they are not phototypeset, spray them with fixative, as they have a tendency to smudge.

Tape the repro securely to a cutting board; using a metal T square, cutting triangle, and single edge razor blade, cut at parallel and right angles to the lines of type. Avoid cutting close to the actual lines of type.

Using tweezers, pick up the type and place it face down. Cover the entire strip and the corresponding area on the mechanical with rubber cement. You will have approximately twenty seconds to position the repro correctly on the mechanical before it dries. If you use one coat of cement you need only apply it to the back of the repro.

If you make a mistake, use rubber cement thinner to lift up the type. Both surfaces must be cleaned before you start again.

Once art is in place, cover it with a piece of tissue paper and press firmly to be certain all areas are pasted down.

If you are using transfer type, remove the protective backing and position the sheet on a piece of paper, aligning the letter with a guideline drawn in blue pencil. Burnish the letter with a ballpoint pen or pencil, using sweeping strokes, and then lift the sheet. Cover the letter with a protective tissue and burnish again to bond letter securely to the paper. The letter will remain on the working surface. If you made a mistake, the letter may be easily removed with a piece of tape. Once you have transferred all necessary letters to a separate piece of paper, treat this sheet as if it were regular type. It is also possible, but not advisable, to transfer type directly to the mechanical. Transfer type may chip and break as you work with it. This tendency can be avoided by treating it with Krylon, a popular brand of spray fixative.

If you find rubber cement difficult to use, other methods are available that allow you to reposition repros or photostats without repasting. An aerosol glue, Spray Mount, may be applied to the back of art or you can roll art with wax by using a special waxing machine.

Pasting Down Halftone Copy

Photographs should not be pasted onto the mechanical as they must be photographed separately through a halftone screen and then stripped into the line negative by the printer. However, the size and position of halftone art must be indicated. This can be done by drawing a red holding line—which will print as black—or by pasting down a photostat. Photostats representing halftones are not shooting copy. "For size and position only" should be written in large clear print across the front of the stat. If holding lines are used, the percentage of enlargement or reduction must be indicated, either by scaling or percentage markings.

Protecting and Marking the Mechanical

When the mechanical is finished, make sure there are no stray marks or glue. Cut a sheet of tracing paper and attach it to the upper edge of the mechanical with masking tape. This protects your mechanical and provides a place to write special instructions to the printer concerning ink color, tint percentages, and reversals of type. Also indicate the paper to be used, the quantity to be printed, and the number to be folded. For added protection, a heavy sheet of paper should be attached over the tracing paper.

Mounting and Marking Shooting Copy

Continuous tone copy (photographs) should be mounted on a piece of artboard with a protective overlay. An identifying number and the percentage of reduction (determined through scaling) should be marked clearly on the board. For example, ''Art A, shoot at 60% of art,'' should be written on the artboard and a corresponding notation should be made on the mechanical.

Do not write on the back of a photograph, as this will make marks that the printer's camera will record. If a photograph must be identified, use a grease crayon. A preferable solution is to type tags and paste them on the back.

Cropmarks should be drawn at all four corners of the photograph. Never cut a photograph or draw cropmarks directly on its surface. Cropmarks may also be indicated by attaching a piece of tracing paper over the surface of the photograph and making appropriate markings.

Always mark the top and bottom of a photograph if there is any doubt as to how it should be positioned.

Proofing Mechanicals

Before a mechanical is delivered to the printer it must be carefully checked and rechecked. If a piece prints on both sides there will be two mechanicals. If it folds, some elements will appear right-side up and some will appear upside down. In reviewing a mechanical be certain that

- All type and art is in its proper place
- There is no dust or dirt on the surface
- There are no typographical errors in the copy
- Artwork is properly labeled

Remember that anything red will print black and that blue lines will not be reproduced in the finished piece.

STEP

6

The Printing

Process

Printing Methods

Bringing the mechanical to the printer represents the final step in the graphic process. Before you have finished your mechanical you should have made arrangements for printing (see page 33). There are several major processes by which your piece can be reproduced, ranging from photocopying to offset lithography. As a rule, offset and duplicators will most effectively meet the printing needs of small organizations working with limited budgets.

Photocopying

Photocopying a flyer is the simplest, cheapest way of reproducing printed material, and because there are copy shops on most street corners, it is the most convenient. Copy quality varies from shop to shop and should be investigated before you place a major order. The cheapest rates can usually be found near university campuses where the proliferation of shops forces operators to keep prices competitive. In recent years copy shops have expanded their services, offering reproductions of photographs and color slides. While photographic quality is inferior to other printing methods, these reproductions can be used to create interesting graphic effects.

Letterpress Printing

Also known as relief printing, Letterpress uses a raised surface to create an image, much like a rubber stamp. Ink comes in contact with raised cast metal type or plates while surrounding nonprint areas are lower and receive no ink. Letterpress is the only process that can use type directly. Although it is still used for small jobs, it has been largely superseded by offset printing.

Gravure

Also known as intaglio printing, Gravure uses a recessed image area plate to create an image. The entire engraved plate is inked, then wiped clean, leaving ink only on the incised area. When printed under pressure this inked area is transferred to the paper. Due to the intricate pla-temaking process, gravure is an extremely expensive process most appropriate for long runs of 500,000 or more.

Offset Lithography

Also referred to as photo-offset or offset, this is the most popular and economical form of printing for most organizations. Today over 75 percent of all printing is done by this process. The printer takes a photograph of the mechanical and screens all continuous tone copy. He/she then "strips" the line and halftone film negatives into a sheet of orange opaque paper, making a flat, which is used to make a printing plate. Offset is based on the principle that grease and water do not mix. The image and the nonprinting area are on the same plane and are differentiated through chemical treatment. The printed image is rendered grease (ink) receptive and water repellent; the nonprinting area is rendered grease repellent and water receptive. The inked image is transferred to a thin rubber blanket wrapped around a press and then "offset" onto the paper that is going through the press. Corrections require the making of new plates, but this can be done relatively quickly and at moderate cost.

Offset presses come in many varieties. The type of press used will be a function of the length of the run, the number of pages, and the number of colors in the job. There are two basic types of offset presses: *web* offset presses that print from paper that is on rolls, and *sheet-fed* presses that print from sheets of paper. Sheet-fed presses best suit the size and scope of print required by most organizations. An offset duplicator—generically known as a Multilith—is a small, relatively unsophisticated, sheet-fed press found in the shops of many neighborhood printers.

In addition to economy and speed, Offset Lithography allows for flexibility in printing because one may erase from the plate. For example, if you wish to code a mail order blank, you can instruct the printer to print several thousand with a code marking and then print the remainder of the run without the marking. Alternatively, if you wish to send some brochures bulk mail and others first class mail, the bulk mail permit can be erased from the plate after the requisite number of bulk mail brochures have been run off.

Reading Blues

Before your piece goes to press the printer will provide you with a blueprint. As the name implies, this is a blue photographic print of your job. It is made from a flat, a series of "stripped up" negatives in which all line and halftone film negatives are assembled in their proper position, as indicated by the mechanical. This is the last time you can make changes before your job goes to press. Corrections will be more expensive at this stage than in any of the previous steps because the printer must strip up a new negative to incorporate alterations. In reading a blueprint check that:

- All photographs are in proper place
- The piece folds correctly
- There are no spots or blemishes on the blueprint
- In a color job, that color placement is correct

Make corrections on the blueprint and return it to the printer. You will be charged additional for anything that is not a printer's error. The printer will then make a printing plate and "run" the job.

Printing the Job

The last stage of the graphic process is the printing and finishing (i.e., binding, folding, and perforating) of your job. If you have carefully followed the procedures outlined in this book it should be printed *on time, on or under budget, and looking good.*

Appendices

Appendix I:
Advertising
Requirements

The preparation of an advertisement, like the preparation of a brochure, must be preceded by a careful and realistic assessment of your organization's needs—what you wish to communicate and to whom, budgetary constraints, and time limitations. The basic steps of design concept, typesetting, and building a mechanical—as outlined in the preceding pages—should be followed. However, because you have no control over the printing process, special factors must be taken into account when planning an advertisement. Just as postal regulations affect the design of a mailer, the requirements of newspapers and magazines dictate aspects of advertisement design.

Design Preliminaries

Before preparing an advertisement call the advertising department of the newspaper or magazine where you wish to have it placed. You will need to find out the following information.

Standard Ad Size

All ads are measured in columns x lines. The width of a column varies from paper to paper. Ad width is an increment of the standard column width of a particular paper plus the space between columns. For example, the column width of *The Village Voice* is 9½ picas or 1⁹⁄₁₆ inches. The required column width for an ad placed in this paper would therefore be as follows:

1 column — 9½ picas wide or 1⁹⁄₁₆″
2 columns — 19½ picas or 3¼″
3 columns — 29½ picas wide or 4⅞″
4 columns — 39½ picas wide or 6⁹⁄₁₆″
5 columns — 49½ picas wide or 8½″
6 columns — 59½ picas wide or 9⅞″

The depth of a column is measured in agate lines. There are 14 agate lines to one inch. All newspapers have minimum depth requirements. After that, ad length increases by the line, with discounts often offered if an ad conforms to a standard size.

Price

Price will probably determine the size ad you decide to run. Cost is based on line rate and is
calculated in lines and columns. A one column ad
of 42 lines would cost the same as a 2 column
ad of 21 lines since both have a total of 42 lines.
To calculate the cost of an ad, ascertain the publication's line rate and multiply the total number of
lines times the rate: number of columns x number
of agate lines x line rate = price of ad.

Line rates vary not only from paper to paper,
but also within the same paper. Variables that
may influence line rate include the section of the
paper in which the ad is placed, the day of the
week on which the ad runs (Sunday is usually
more expensive), the frequency with which the
advertiser places ads with the publication, the
number of times the ad will run over a given period of time, and the type of organization placing
the ad.

Halftone Screen Requirements

In order to print a photograph, the image must be
broken into a series of dots through screening
(see page 69). When you prepare a brochure, the
printer screens the halftone, but when you submit
an ad to a newspaper, photographs often must
be screened in advance. Screens come in varying coarsenesses, depending on the absorbency

of the paper and the printing process employed. Newspapers use coarser screens (fewer dots per inch) than magazines. The *New York Times* requires 65 line screens. *The Village Voice* requires a screen of 85 lines. Some newspapers also require that large blocks of solid color be screened.

Deadlines

Publications have two deadlines for placing advertisements—one for reserving space and one for submitting artwork. Reservations for space can be made over the telephone. Deadlines for weeklies are usually at least one and a half weeks before publication date.

Other Requirements

Check to see if a publication has any special requirements. For example, mechanicals for ads are usually mounted on illustration board, but some newspapers require that ads be unmounted. Many papers require that reverses be screened.

Preparing the Mechanical

The mechanical you submit to a publication should be camera ready. That means it should look exactly as it will look when it is printed and should be the same size as the ad that will appear in the paper. All halftones should be screened.

Once you have determined the size of your ad, set up a proportional space on your mechanical by using a proportion wheel. Your mechanical should have the same relative dimensions as your final ad so that when you take it to the photostat house it can be properly reduced.

Keep your ad clear and simple. Remember that it is competing with many other ads and news items.

To save time and money and to give your promotional material a unified design sense, you may wish to incorporate elements from a flyer, brochure, or stationery into your mechanical. Keep in mind, however, that if you reduce your mechanical, type and artwork will be reduced proportionately. Type should not be reduced beyond 10 points or readability will be impaired. If you use reverses or very thin typefaces, type should be larger.

If your ad does not meet a publication's typographical standards, the publication usually converts the artwork as necessary and bills you additionally.

Proofing the Mechanical

In checking your mechanical, be certain it contains all relevant information. For a performance or special event this includes:

- Day, date, and time of event
- Ticket price (including discounts)
- Address
- Name of event
- Box office telephone number

For a product or service:

- Clear identification of item being offered
- Address or phone number for obtaining additional information.

Pub Setting Ads

If you are working with a limited budget you can let the publication typeset your ad, rather than preparing your own mechanical. You supply them with typed copy and a sketch of the layout. The major disadvantage of pub setting is that it gives you less control over the final product and little protection against errors. It also limits your selection of typefaces.

Delivering Your Mechanical

When you submit your advertisement it should be accompanied by an insertion order specifying the size of the ad, the date it is to run, and the section of the paper in which it is to run. You cannot reserve a specific spot in the paper unless you are willing to pay a premium.

Appendix II: Postal Regulations

By sending flyers or brochures bulk mail at third class rates, your organization can save significantly on mailing costs. However, it is essential that you strictly adhere to the U.S. Postal Regulations concerning such mailing. Failure to observe any of the regulations may result in the rejection of your entire mailing. Some of the postal regulations affect the design and printing of a mailing piece; others concern how the mailing is carried out (zipcoding, bundling, and so on). Those that affect printing and design are discussed below.

3rd Class Mailing Permit

In order to take advantage of the reduced rates of bulk mailing you must have a 3rd class mailing permit. This can be obtained at the General Post Office. Special discount rates are available to not-for-profit organizations. To obtain such a permit, you must present the following materials:

- Federal Income Tax Exemption
- Certificate of Incorporation showing goals and purposes
- Brochure or literature showing goals and purposes
- Brochure or literature describing your organization's activities
- Payment—a) $40.00 yearly fee and b) $40.00 one-time permit fee for permit number (automatically renewable without additional charge if used at least once in a twelve month period).

Postage for bulk mailing must be prepaid by either meter stamps, precancelled stamps, precancelled stamped envelopes, or permit imprints. Most organizations use permit imprints, also known as indicias, for their bulk mailings. In addition to the permit number, not-for-profit organizations must include the words "NOT-FOR-PROFIT ORGANIZATION" or "NOT-FOR-PROFIT ORG" on the first line of the indicia.

Placement of Indicia

The indicia should be placed in the upper right corner, parallel to the longer side of the mailer.

Size Regulations

Cards and folded flyers can be no larger than
11½″ × 13½″ and the post office recommends
that they not exceed 9″ × 12″ to insure easy
handling. Pieces should be no smaller than 3½″
× 5″; they must weigh less than 2.8 ounces and
be less than ¼″ thick.

Design of Address Space

Mailers must leave at least 3½ inches from the
top and 3½ inches from the right clear space for
address information. Mailers larger than letter size
must leave 3 inches from the top and 4¼ inches
from the right clear space.

Color

Very pale or brilliantly colored ink should be
avoided for the printing of logo, indicia, or address, as should brilliantly colored paper. The
post office can reject a piece based on color, so
if you think your color choice may cause prob-
lems, bring a sample to the post office for
approval.

   *Please note, that the federal government is
currently reevaluating its bulk mail, not-for-profit
rates and the system may soon undergo signifi-
cant changes. Contact the central post office in
your community before proceeding with a mailing.*

Appendix III: Comparative Cost Chart

Subscription Brochure
Specifications given to printer:

Quantity: 75,000, plus cost of additional 5,000
Stock (paper): 60, 70, 0r 80 pound coated offset
Colors: 1, 2, 3, or 4 flat colors
Size: 12½ x 18; folds twice to 9 x 6¼
Delivery: Manhattan
Halftones: 3, approx. 4" x 6" each; one is a silhouette

PRINTER A

		1 Color	2 Color	3 Color	4 Color
60 lb.		$3,730	$4,100	$5,050	$5,299
	add'l. 5,000	422	470	517	517
70 lb.		4,150	4,520	5,470	5,740
	add'l. 5,000	470	490	560	560
80 lb.		4,935	4,940	5,890	6,160
	add'l. 5,000	530	530	603	603

PRINTER B

		1 Color	2 Color	3 Color	4 Color
60 lb.		$2,540	$2,940	$3,547	$3,836
	add'l. 5,000	290	305	364	398
70 lb.		2,964	3,430	4,138	4,475
	add'l. 5,000	338	356	425	465
80 lb.		3,387	3,920	4,729	5,115
	add'l. 5,000	386	407	485	532

PRINTER C

		1 Color	2 Color	3 Color	4 Color
60 lb.		$4,247	$4,572	$5,492	$5,492
	add'l. 5,000	242	242	322	322
70 lb.		4,515	4,840	5,760	5,760
	add'l. 5,000	260	260	340	340
80 lb.		4,783	5,108	6,028	6,028
	add'l. 5,000	278	278	358	358

Appendix IV: Literature

More detailed information on graphic design, typesetting, and printing may be found in the publications listed below. The American Institute of Graphic Arts (1059 Third Avenue, New York, NY) maintains an extensive library of graphic arts books.

Ballingen, Raymond. LAYOUT AND GRAPHIC DE-
SIGN. New York: Van Nostrand Reinhold, 1980.
Burke, Clifford. PRINTING IT: A GUIDE TO GRAPHIC
TECHNIQUES FOR THE IMPECUNIOUS. Berkley:
Book People, 1976.
Craig, James. DESIGNING WITH TYPE——A BASIC
COURSE IN TYPOGRAPHY. New York: Watson-
Guptil, 1971.

Craig, James. PRODUCTION FOR THE GRAPHIC DE-
SIGNER. New York: Watson-Guptil, 1974.

Goodchild, Jon and Henkin, Bill. BY DESIGN: A
GRAPHIC SOURCEBOOK OF MATERIALS,
EQUIPMENT, AND SERVICES. New York: Quick
Fox, 1979.

GRAPHIC COMMUNICATIONS FOR THE PERFORM-
ING ARTS. New York: Theatre Communications
Group, 1981.

GRAPHIC STANDARDS MANUAL. Denver: Colorado
Council on the Arts and Humanities, 1980.

POCKET PAL. International Paper Company, 1973.

Laundry, Peter and Vignelli, Massimo. GRAPHIC DE-
SIGN FOR NON-PROFIT ORGANIZATIONS. New
York: American Institute for Graphic Arts, 1980.

Ruder, Emil. TYPOGRAPHY. New York: Visual Communications Books. Hastings, 1967.

Smith, Ray. AIGA GRAPHIC DESIGN USA: 1. New
York: Watson-Guptil, 1981.

Snyder, John. COMMERCIAL ARTISTS HANDBOOK.
New York: Watson-Guptil, 1973.

Glossary

AA: Author's alteration, any changes or additions to copy after it has been set that are not due to printer's errors. These alterations are charged additional.

Accordian Fold: Two or more parallel folds of paper which open like an accordian.

Against the Grain: Folding paper at right angles to the grain.

Agate: Unit of measure used in newspapers to calculate column space: 14 agate lines equal one inch.

Antique Finish: Usually applied to book and cover papers with a natural, rough finish.

Art: All copy used in preparing a job—photographs, illustrations, type.

Ascender: The part of a lowercase letter that rises above the body of a letter, as in ''b,'' ''f,'' and ''k.''

Author's Alteration: See ''AA.''

B

Backing-Up: Printing the reverse side of a sheet already printed on one side.

Bad Break: In composition, when the first line of a page is hyphenated. Also, incorrect end-of-line hyphenation.

Basis Weight: Weight in pounds of 500 sheets (a ream) of paper cut to a given standard size for that grade.

Benday Screen: A screen that prints inks at percentage of their full color, thus allowing for the introduction of tonalities into a piece: a benday screen of black produces grey, of red produces pink.

BF: Boldface.

Bleed: Area of a plate that extends—or ''bleeds''—beyond the edge to be trimmed. Usually refers to photographs or areas of color. When a design involves a bleed, ⅛'' to ¼'' must be allowed beyond the trim size. Printers must use slightly larger sheets to accommodate bleeds.

Blow-Up: An enlargement of copy including photographs, artwork, or type.

Blueprints: In offset-lithography or photoengraving, a photoprint made from stripped-up negatives or positives, used as a proof to check the position of artwork and type.

Body: In composition, the metal block of a piece of type that carries the printing surface.

Body Type: Type, from 6 points to 14 points, used for the main part or text of a printed piece, as distinguished from headings.

Boldface: A heavier version of a regular typeface indicated as BF.

Bulk: The thickness of a paper, measured in pages per inch (PPI).

Bullet: Large dot used as a design device.

Burnish: A rubbing motion used to smooth down self-adhering letters.

C

Calligraphy: Elegant handwriting or personalized scripts.

Caps and Small Caps: Two sizes of capital letters on one typeface, the small caps being the same size as the body of the lowercase letters. Indicated as C & S.C.

Character Count: The number of characters in a line, paragraph, or piece of copy.

Characters-Per-Pica (CPP): System of copyfitting that uses the average number of characters per pica as a means of determining the length of copy when set in type.

Coated Paper: Paper having a surface coating that produces a smooth finish, providing a surface especially suited for reproducing halftones.

Cold Type: Type set by a direct impression method. Also known as strike-on composition.

Color Matching System: Method of specifying flat color by means of numbered color samples. Available in swatchbooks. Popularly known as PMS, or Pantone Matching System.

Color Separation: The process of separating art-work into four primary process colors in negative or positive form, by photographing through filters or by electronic scanners. These films are then scanned to make printing plates.

Comp: Short for comprehensive sketch. A layout prepared by the designer for the client indicating the layout of type and illustrations.

Continuous Tone Copy: An image with a full range of tones from black to white such as photographs or charcoal drawings.

Contrast: Tonal gradations, usually of photographic originals or reproductions.

Comprehensive Sketch: See ''Comp.''

Cool Colors: Blue, green, and violet, as opposed to warm colors, red, yellow, and orange.

Copy: In design and typesetting, typewritten copy. In printing, all artwork——type, photographs, and illustrations——to be printed.

Copyfitting: Determining the amount of manu-script copy that can fit into a given area for a specified size and style of type.

Cover Paper: Term applied to a variety of papers used for the covers of brochures, catalogues, and booklets.

Crop: To eliminate portions of copy, usually on photographs.

Cropmarks: In design, the lines drawn on a overlay or in the margins of a photograph to indicate to the printer where the image should be trimmed.

Descenders: The part of a lower case letter that falls below the body of a letter as in "g," "j," "p," "q," and "y."

Display Type: Type that is set larger than the text. Usually 18 points or larger. It is used to attract attention.

Dots: Minute elements that make up a halftone.

Double Dot Duotone: A duotone in which both plates are printed in black.

Double Dot Halftone: Two halftone negatives combined into one printing plate, producing a printed reproduction with a greater tonal range. One negative reproduces highlights and shadows, the other reproduces middletones.

Dropout Halftone: A halftone in which the highlight areas have no screen dots so that all that appears in the highlight areas is the white of the paper.

Duotone: A two-color halftone reproduced from a one-color photograph. One plate is made for the black, picking up highlight and shadow areas; a second plate is made for the second color, picking up the middletones.

Family of Type: All the type sizes and styles of a particular type face (Roman, Italic, Bold, and so on).

First Proofs: Proofs submitted for checking by proofreaders, copy editors, and so forth.

Flat: An assemblage of various film negatives or positives attached to a piece of film, goldenrod, or masking material ready to be exposed to a plate. Also, a photograph or halftone lacking in contrast.

Flat Color: Solid colors and tints other than process color. Flat color is usually printed as 1,2,3, or 4 color jobs.

Flop: To turn over an image so that it faces the opposite way.

Flush Left (or Right): In composition, type set to line up at the left (or right).

Folio: Page number.

Font: Complete assortment of type of one size and face.

Four Color Process: Method of producing full-color copy by separating the color image into its three primary colors—magenta, yellow, cyan—plus black. This results in four printing plates, one for each color, which when printed one over the other, produces the effect of all the colors in the original art.

French Fold: A double fold in which the sheet is folded once vertically and once horizontally.

Galley Proof: Also called rough proof. An impression of type that allows the client to see that the job has been properly set.

Gang Printing: Running off any different number of jobs on the same sheet.

Grain: Predominant direction of the fibers in a sheet of paper.

Halftone: The photographic reproduction of continuous tone copy, such as photographs, through a screen that converts the image into dots of different sizes.

Halftone Negative: The negative film produced

by shooting continuous tone copy through a half-tone screen.

Halftone Positive: A photographic positive containing screened continuous tone copy in the form of dots.

Hickey: A defect or spot appearing in a printed piece usually caused by dirt on the pages, dried ink skin, or paper particles.

Holding Lines: Lines drawn on the mechanical by the designer to indicate the exact area to be occupied by a halftone, color, tint, and so on.

Hot Type: Type produced by casting hot metal.

Imposition: The arrangement of pages in a press form so that they will appear in correct order after the printed sheet is folded.

Indicia: Information printed by special permit on cards or envelopes that takes the place of a stamp.

Justified Type: Lines of type that align on both the left and the right.

L

Laquer: A clear coating, usually glossy, applied to a printed sheet for protection or appearance.

Lamination: A plastic film bonded, by heat and pressure, to a printed sheet for protection or appearance.

L.C.: Abbreviation for lower case, the small letters of type as distinguished from capital letters.

Leading: The space between lines of type.

Letraset: Brand name of transfer type.

Letterpress: A printing method in which a raised image area is inked by a roller and the image is transferred directly to paper by pressure.

Letterspacing: The placing of additional space between letters in order to fill out a line of type to a given measure or to improve appearance.

Line Art: Artwork consisting of solid blacks and whites, with no tonal values.

Line Conversion: The conversion of continuous tone copy to line copy through the use of halftone screens to create special effects.

Line Copy: Any copy suitable for reproduction without using a halftone screen. Line copy is solid black with no gradations of tones.

Lithography: A planographic printing method in which the image area is separated from the non-image by chemical repulsion.

Logo Type (or "Logo"): A joining of characters as a trademark or company signature.

Lower Case: Small letters as opposed to capitals, abbreviated l.c.

M

Make Ready: In printing, all the work done to prepare the press prior to actually running the job.

Master: A plate for a duplicating machine.

Matte Finish: Dull paper finish without gloss or lustre.

Mechanical: An assembly of all type and design elements pasted on artboard or illustration board in exact position and containing instructions, either in the margins or on a tissue overlay, for the printer.

Moire Pattern: An undesirable pattern that occurs when art that has been photographed through a halftone screen is rescreened.

Multilith: Trade name for a small offset duplicator

used for small jobs such as envelopes, forms, cards, and letterheads.

Negative: A reverse photographic image on film or paper.

O

Offset Lithography: Commonly called offset. A printing method in which the image and non-image areas are separated by chemical means based on the principle that grease and water do not mix. The ink is transferred from the plate onto a rubber blanket and then onto the paper.

Opacity: The quality in a sheet of paper that prevents the type on one side from showing through to the other.

Overage: Copies printed in excess of specified quantities. Also known as overrun.

Overlay: Transparent paper or film placed over artwork for protection or for indicating instructions to the printer.

Overrun: See overage.

Pantone Matching System: Brand name for a widely used color matching system. Also known as PMS.

Paper Grades: Categories of paper based on such characteristics as size, weight, and grain.

Photo Mechanical Transfer (PMT): A direct positive made by a photostat house.

PE: Printer's error. A mistake made by the printer, as opposed to an "AA."

Photostat: Also known as a stat. Commonly used in mechanicals to indicate size and position of photographs..

Phototypesetting: The method of setting type photographically by projecting images onto photosensitive paper or film.

Pica: A typographic unit of measurement: 12 points = 1 pica; 6 picas = 1 inch.

PMS: See "Pantone Matching System."

Point: A unit of measure used to designate type size: 12 points = 1 pica, 72 points = 1 inch.

Positive: A photographic reproduction on paper, film, or glass that corresponds to the original. The reverse of a negative.

Press Proof: A proof pulled on the actual production press (as opposed to a proofing press) to show how the piece will look when printed. Press proofs are usually checked right at the printing plant.

Press Run: The length of the run or the number of sheets to be printed.

Printer's Error: See "PE."

Printing Plate: A surface, usually made of metal, that has been treated to carry an image. The plate is inked and the ink is transferred to the paper or other surface by a printing press.

Process Color: The reproduction of color by use of four separate printing plates, one for each of the primary colors—magenta (process red), yellow, and cyan (process blue)—and one for black.

Progressive Proofs: Proofs made in color process work showing each color printed alone and in sequential combination with other colors.

Proofs: A print of typeset material that is checked against the original manuscript and upon which corrections are made.

Ream: 500 sheets of paper.

Reproduction Proof: Also called a "repro." A

proof made from type ready to be pasted into the mechanical and reproduced photographically.

Repro: See ''Reproduction Proof.''

Reverse: Type that drops out of the background and assumes the color of the paper.

Right-Angle Fold: Folds that are at 90 degrees to each other.

Rough: A sketch giving a general idea of the size and position of the elements in a design.

Rough Proof: Any proof pulled from type on a proofing press.

Scaling: The process of calculating the percentage of enlargement or reduction of original artwork.

Screen: The contact or crossline screen placed before the lens of a camera to break up continuous tone copy (photographs) into dots for reproduction. Screens come in varying coarsenesses.

Self-Mailer: A printed piece designed to be mailed without an envelope.

Shooting Copy: Copy ready to be shot by the printer in order to make a plate.

Silhouette Halftone: A halftone reproduction in which the main image area is outlined by removing the dots that surround it.

Spec.: To specify to the typesetter how type should be set.

Strike-On Composition: Type set by a direct impression or on a typewriter composing machine. Also known as cold type.

Stripping: In offset lithography, the positioning of negatives (or positives) on a flat prior to plate-making.

Text: The body matter of a page or book as distinguished from headlines.

Tints: Various even tone areas of a solid color created by screening.

Tone: The variation in a color or the range of grays between black and white.

Trim Marks: Marks placed on a mechanical to indicate the edge of the page.

Trim Size: The final size of a printed piece.

Typographic Errors: Commonly called "typos." Errors made in copy while typing either at a conventional typewriter, or by the compositor when setting type. Typos made by the compositor are "PE's" and are not charged to the client.

U & L.C.: Abbreviation for upper and lower case.

Uncoated Paper: A basic paper made without coating.

Unjustified Type: Lines of type set at different lengths that align on either the left or right and are ragged on the other side.

Upper Case: The capital letters of a type font.

V

Velox: A high quality screened photostat that can be used in the preparation of mechanicals and shot along with line art.

Warm Colors: Red, yellow, and orange. As opposed to cold colors, blue, green, and violet.

Web Press: A press which prints from rolls (or webs) or paper.

With the Grain: Folding paper parallel to the grain.

Index